Contents

Any words appearing in the text in bold, **like this**, are explained in the glossary.

This is Australia

The country of Australia is an island. In fact, it is the largest island in the world. Australia is also one of the world's seven **continents**, or great landmasses.

If you took your camera to Australia, you could take photographs of many things.

Perth is the largest city on Australia's west coast. Much of the country's wheat is grown on land near Perth.

In Australia's countryside, you might see large ranches where sheep and cattle are raised. You may even see **koalas** eating the leaves of **eucalyptus**, or gum, trees.

Australia has many large cities, like Sydney, Melbourne and Perth. Melbourne is Australia's second largest city. It is known for its skyscrapers and for its lovely city parks.

This book will show you some of these places. It will also tell you much about Australia. If you learn about Australia before you take your camera there, you will enjoy your visit more.

Koalas are one of the many animals found only in Australia.

The place

Australia is the smallest **continent**, but it is a huge country. It is nearly 3220 kilometres (2000 miles) from north to south and about 3860 kilometres (2400 miles) from east to west. Australia is about the size of the USA.

Australia is far away from most other places. It takes more than a day to fly to the city of Sydney from London. Australia is so far south that sometimes it is referred to as 'Down Under'. Being an island, Australia is completely surrounded by water. The Timor and Arafura seas are to the north. The **Coral** Sea is to the north-east. The eastern part of Australia touches the Pacific Ocean, and on the south and west is the Indian Ocean. Australia's coastline is 25,760 kilometres (16,010 miles) long. The nearest landmass is Papua New Guinea.

Tasmania is a small island off Australia's south coast. It is part of Australia.

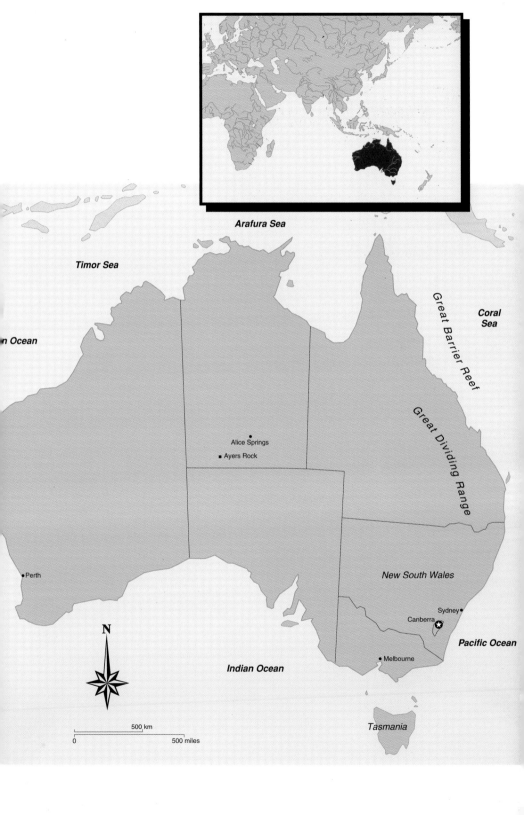

Arafura Sea

Timor Sea

Ocean

Coral
Sea

Great Barrier Reef

Great Dividing Range

Alice Springs
■ Ayers Rock

• Perth

New South Wales

Sydney •
Canberra ☆

Pacific Ocean

N

• Melbourne

Indian Ocean

500 km
0   500 miles

Tasmania

Most of Australia is flat, with many deserts. Australia's one mountain range, the Great Dividing Range, stretches down the eastern side of the country from north to south. The highest mountain is Mount Kosciusko, at 2230 metres high.

Because Australia is south of the **equator**, the seasons are the reverse of those north of it. Summer in Australia is from December to February, and winter is from June to August.

It is very hot in the north, but milder in the south. In the hottest parts temperatures of 37°C (100°F) have been recorded.

Some Australian cattle ranches cover thousands of square km.

Bondi Beach is a very popular beach located near Sydney.

The north and north-east coasts are the wettest, with 100 to 200 centimetres of rain every year. In Sydney the rainfall is about 100 centimetres a year. In the deserts, there may be as little as 15 centimetres of rain a year and in many years there may be no rain at all. Australia has many wind storms, dust storms and cyclones every year. Cyclones are very strong windstorms.

Sydney

Sydney is Australia's oldest, largest and most important city. It is the capital of a state of Australia known as New South Wales. Sydney was first settled in 1788.

Sydney has one of the best harbours in the world. It is also a busy one. Sydney has two famous landmarks. The Sydney Harbour Bridge was built in 1932 and is 503 metres long. The other famous sight is the Sydney Opera House, which was completed in 1973.

This beautiful building looks like a set of huge, wind-filled sails.

People who live in Sydney and its nearby suburbs use trains and buses to get to work every day. Because Sydney is built on the water, **commuters** also use fast boats and ferries. Like most modern cities, Sydney can have plenty of traffic jams during the daily rush hours. Most people who live in Sydney work in the **manufacturing** and tourist **industries**.

Botany Bay is near Sydney. The English explorer named Captain James Cook landed there in 1770. So many kinds of plants and flowers were growing there that one of his crew named the bay 'Botany'. Today it is part of Sydney's suburbs.

Sydney Harbour at night with two of Australia's best-known landmarks: the Sydney Opera House and behind it the Sydney Harbour Bridge.

Places to visit

The Great Barrier Reef is the world's largest **coral** reef. A reef is a chain of coral near the surface of the water. The Great Barrier Reef is located near the north-east coast of Australia. It is made up of about 500 small islands and coral reefs. About 400 types of coral and 1500 types of fish live in the clear, warm water.

People come to the Great Barrier Reef to swim and snorkel so they can watch the rich variety of wildlife.

Uluru is important to Australia's native people. It is also known as Ayers Rock.

Another of Australia's famous natural landmarks is Uluru, also known as Ayers Rock. It is a great red slab of rock that rises about 335 metres above the flat desert in central Australia. Parts of the rock and its caves are decorated with drawings that are very old. The **Aboriginal** people drew graceful images of animals in charcoal and then coloured them with chalk and clay.

Alice Springs is a town almost in the centre of the country, about 450 kilometres (280 miles) north-east of Uluru. Visitors go there because it looks almost exactly like it did when it was first settled about 150 years ago.

The people

About 19 million people live in Australia. That is fewer people than in most countries of its size. Almost all Australians have ancestors who came from other countries, starting about 200 years ago. About 92 per cent are Europeans, or have European ancestors. The, first Europeans to settle in Australia were from the United Kingdom. About 7 per cent of Australians today are Asian.

An even smaller number are **Aborigines**. This is the name early European settlers gave to the native people

The Aborigines have been in Australia for more than 40,000 years.

who were already living in Australia. The word *Aborigine* means 'from the beginning'. For many years these people were nomads. This means they wandered from place to place. When European settlers came, they took land away from the Aborigines. Recent laws have been passed that give the Aborigines more rights to the land.

The vast majority of the Australian population lives along its coastline.

Life in Australia

Most Australians live in cities. In cities, some Australians live in flats, but most people like to live in houses. Three-quarters of Australians own their own homes. Many of the houses have small, well-tended gardens. Some also have **verandas** and swimming pools. New suburbs surround the larger cities. Most Australian cities are modern-looking, with tall skyscrapers. Because Australia is a fairly new country, there are very few old buildings.

Some Australians live on ranches, or stations. Often stations are far from one another. In fact, the distances are often so great between places in Australia that doctors use helicopters and small planes to visit patients.

Most people in Australia live near the country's coasts. The outback and the bush begin away from the coast, in the interior.

Outback is the name given to those parts of Australia that are isolated and **rural**. The bush is the area in Australia that has trees and woods.

Even today there are few roads in much of the centre of Australia. There are also areas there that have never been fully explored.

Kangaroos live only in Australia. They move by jumping on their strong hind legs.

Many people like Australia's unique animal and plant life. One unusual animal that lives only in Australia is the kangaroo. In some areas there are too many kangaroos so people hunt them to control their numbers.

Computers and good telephone systems make distances between sheep and cattle stations seem smaller.

17

Government and religion

Australia has a democratic federal government. 'Democratic' means that Australia's leaders are elected. 'Federal' means that Australia is made up of a group of separate states that have joined together under one government. The country is made up of six states and two territories. Queen Elizabeth II is the official head of state, but she does not play any part in Australian politics. The queen's representative in Australia is called the governor-general. The prime minister is the real head of government. He or she is elected by the citizens of Australia.

Canberra is the capital of Australia. It is a small city that is part of the Australian Capital Territory. Canberra was created specially to be Australia's capital city. Although it is the country's capital, Canberra is much smaller than Sydney or Melbourne.

Government buildings in Canberra, Australia's capital.

Many of Australia's people are Christians. About half of them are **Protestant** and about a quarter are **Roman Catholics**. Roman Catholics are the most active, and attend weekly services. Most Roman Catholics send their children to religious schools.

There are some **Jews** and Muslims. Muslims follow the teachings of Mohammed. Their religion is called Islam.

19

Earning a living

Australia is large and still growing, so there are plenty of jobs for most people.

Only about 5 per cent of Australia's workers are farmers. Because much of the land is so dry, only about 10 per cent of it can be used for farming. Wheat, barley, oats and sugarcane are grown, as well as grapes, maize and other fruits and vegetables.

Raising cattle, sheep and pigs is very important to the Australian economy. About 30 per cent of the world's supply of wool comes from Australia's sheep. Beef, lamb, wool and wheat are Australia's chief exports, or goods that are sent out of the country to be sold in another.

Australia's main **industries** are iron, steel, cloth, electrical equipment, chemicals and machinery. Making cars, aircraft and ships is also important. Australia's **natural resources** include **bauxite**, coal, copper, iron, lead, tin, **uranium** and **zinc**. Gold, diamonds and opals are among the country's more valuable resources. Oil and natural gas are major industries. They continue to grow larger each year.

Many people come to Australia for long visits. They are eager to see some of Australia's unique animal and plant life. As a result, tourism is growing each year. About a third of Australians work in the tourist industry.

This Australian industrial worker is wearing protective clothing.

Schools and sport

Children in Australia have to go to school between the ages of six and fifteen. In remote areas, children may get their lessons from the School of the Air. Teachers teach their classes by two-way radio. Students ask their questions and teachers answer them by radio. In this way teachers can reach students spread out over hundreds of square kilometres.

There are more than twenty universities in Australia, including Sydney University and Melbourne University.

Because Australia has a warm and sunny climate, outdoor sports are extremely popular. Some sports came with the settlers from the United Kingdom many years ago and are still popular. Cricket, rugby and golf are among these. Australians who live near the coast especially like to go swimming and surfing. Many people enjoy hunting and fishing.

Water sports are very popular along Australia's coasts.

Food and Festivals

Much of the cooking in Australia is based on the dishes brought by the first settlers from the United Kingdom. Australians eat a lot of beef and lamb, products of the cattle and sheep they raise. Like many people around the world, however, Australians are cutting back on the amount of red meat they eat. People are trying to eat more fresh vegetables and fruit.

Australians are outdoor people, and they enjoy barbecued food. They like to set up grills and cook steaks or fish in their back gardens. They can also dine out at many of the larger cities' fine restaurants. More recent peoples who have come to Australia, such as Asians, have brought their own foods and recipes to the country.

Some Australians hold Christmas parties on the beach.

As in the United Kingdom, Christmas is one of the most important festivals. Because Christmas comes during Australia's summer, Australians think of this festival as a time of warm sunshine and growing flowers. Easter comes in Australia's autumn.

25

The future

Because Australia is a fairly new country, there is room for much growth. Modern **technology** is ideal for helping Australia develop. Telephones, faxes, computers and especially the Internet and e-mail solve the problems of great distances in this huge country.

Like many large countries, Australia has some problems. Although there are a lot of jobs for people, many of them are part-time jobs. But there is little crime and very little pollution in Australia. Australians are proud of their many unique plants and animals and are taking care to protect them. Australians have set aside many national parks and animal reserves.

Australians are trying to improve the lives of the country's original people. It is hoped that the future will bring more understanding of the **Aborigines**. This will lead to a greater appreciation of

their ancient culture, which is one of the world's oldest.

A typical Australian greeting is 'Good day, mate'. With the Australian accent, it sounds more like 'G-day, might'.

Modern technology helps Australians keep in touch with one another and the rest of the world.

Quick facts about
AUSTRALIA

Capital
Canberra

Borders
Indian Ocean
Pacific Ocean

Area
7,682,850 square kilometres
(2,966,136 square miles)

Population ▶
19.3 million

◀ **Largest cities**
Sydney (3,719,000 people);
Melbourne (3,187,500 people);
Canberra (325,400 people)

Main crops
wheat, barley, sugar cane, fruit,
livestock, grapes

Natural resources
bauxite, coal, iron ore, copper, tin

Longest river
Murray, at 2589 km (1609 miles)

Flag of Australia

Coastline
25,760 km (16,010 miles)

Monetary unit
Australian dollar

Literacy rate
99 per cent of Australians can read and write.

Major industries
mining, industrial and transport equipment, food processing

29

Glossary

Aborigines (ah-buh-RIJI-neez) native people who have lived in Australia for perhaps 40,000 years. The word means 'from the beginning'.

bauxite (BOARK-zite) rock involved in the extraction of aluminium

botany science that studies plants

continent one of the world's seven main continuous stretches of land

commuter person who travels regularly to work

coral hard external skeleton that serves as a shelter for certain small creatures that live in the sea

equator imaginary line around the centre of the Earth that divides it into two equal parts

eucalyptus group of evergreen trees that originates from Australia and is the main type of tree there

industry making of goods or products

Jew (JOO) follower of Judaism, a religion that believes in one God and awaits the coming of a saviour, or Messiah

koala (koe-WA-la) mammal that lives on eucalyptus leaves and is only found in Australia. Koalas raise their young in a pouch on the mother's belly.

manufacture produce something in a factory out of other materials

natural resources things from nature that are useful to people

Protestant Christian church that broke away from the Catholic Church in the 16th century

Roman Catholic Christian church, based in Rome, Italy, that considers the Pope to be Christ's representative on Earth

rural undeveloped countryside

technology advances in science applied to practical problems and daily life

uranium (yew-RAIN-ee-um) radioactive metal that is used to produce nuclear energy and nuclear weapons

veranda (veh-RAN-dah) roofed platform outside a house, level with the ground floor

zinc silvery-white metal used to make brass

Index